The Face Behind MS

My Journey

By Lisa Norman

Heart Ink Press LLC

Since 2009

Tallahassee • Plant City

ISBN 978-0-9835854-7-3

Heart.Ink Press
www.heartinkpress.com
Tuned to the beat of your heart
Manifesting dreams and visions

Printed in the United States of America

Dedicated to

I would like to dedicate this book to my Lord and Savior Jesus Christ who anointed me with the gift of writing, and blessed me with 2 exceptional daughters (Shannel and Cierra). Although I was the person diagnosed with MS, it was as if we were intertwined; going through this as one. Shannel you are my oldest and you had to endure my insensitivity the longest. Especially during the times when you needed me, you unselfishly denied yourself and became the strength and support I needed. I am very remorseful for that and I cannot bring back the past, but I want you to know I thank you and love you more than words can ever say. To my youngest daughter, Cierra, you had an advisor in Shannel to try and walk you through the adversity, but it does not mean you did not feel the consequence of what I was going through. I appreciate your willingness to unite with your sister in trying to stay afloat with this situation. I am very regretful for all the confusion that I caused you and I love you very much. The both of you have and will always be The Face Behind My MS.

Acknowledgements

In loving memory of my Mother, Louise, and my brother, Curtis, who had always let me know that with GOD all things are possible.

Words cannot express my gratitude to Editor Chakita Hargrove for her professional advice and assistance in polishing my manuscript.

This book would not have been possible without the love and support of my daughters, Shannel and Cierra.

In appreciation to my sisters, Harriett who kindly suggested the title for my book, Renee whose vision impelled me to keep writing, Eartha for encouraging me not give up, and Janet for believing in me.

I express thanks to my nephew Nick and his wife Erica for referring me to Chakita Hargrove.

For understanding my long nights at the computer I would like to thank my grandson Daniel.

Thanks to my cousin Shelitha for always being there and to my friend Tammy for her considerate book review.

I appreciate the caring counsel from all others mentioned in the book.

Table of Contents

<u>UNKNOWN BEGINNINGS</u>

Let me introduce myself. My name is Lisa Norman.

My mother Louise had six amazing children; Janet, Eartha, Harriett, Renee, Curtis, and Lisa. I was the youngest, but I was the biggest in birth weight. I weighed a sizeable 8 pounds at birth and I arrived one month earlier than the doctors predicted.

After my birth, the doctor informed my mother that I was a nervous baby and to avoid making any piercing noises when I was around. Listening to the doctor's advice my mother would remove me from the room when she had friends or family over; she knew they could sometimes become noisy.

I never crawled as a baby, but I began to walk at 6 months. As I grew older I used to always complain to my mother that my arm was hurting. I was too young to give her an exact explanation of the pain so she would often end up taking me to the hospital.

The doctors could never find anything wrong. We would always get sent home completely clueless about the cause of the pain. The only medical condition my mother ever mentioned to me was having walking pneumonia when I was three-years-old. She had informed me that I had lost a lot of weight after my bout with the illness.

As a kid I enjoyed playing on the swing set we had in our backyard. I played on it almost every day. One afternoon, when I was around 8-9 years old, I decided to play on the monkey bars. I wrapped my legs across the bar hanging myself upside down and I fell.

I hit my head hard on the ground. I started trying to remember my name and address to make sure I did not have a concussion. There was nothing wrong with my memory, but my head was hurting for awhile. I did not tell my mother I had fallen. I simply told her that I had a headache just so I could get an aspirin and go back outside.

It wasn't until I was between 10- 12-years-old when for the first time I had experienced an unusual pain in my leg. The driveway to my house had a metal fence that separated the driveway from the backyard. It was a double fence with a latch in the middle that kept one side closed as you would go through the other side.

I used to always open the latch to walk to the other side, but one day I decided not to open the latch. Instead I jumped over the fence. When my feet touched the ground a sharp awful pain went through my leg.

This was not the "you broke your leg" type of pain; because I knew what a broken leg looked like. This pain was more excruciating than that. It had me so baffled to where I thought "what the hell was that?" I stood there for a while until the feeling returned in my leg. From that moment on I made a point to always open the latch to walk through. The thought of this incident had always seemed very peculiar to me.

When I was in middle school, between 12- 14-years-old, I had this bothersome pain that would come and go in my leg. With no idea of what it could be, I made up my own method of how I would deal with the problem to make it go away.

During the winter I found that sitting beside the heater when the pain was happening seemed to make the pain go away. At other times I would hit on my leg and tell whatever was in there to get out. Neither of those remedies really worked. The pain continued to annoy me.

I finally told my parents about the warm and itchy pain that I had felt in my leg. My parents took me to an Urgent Care Center. I told the doctor everything I had told my parents. The only question the doctor asked me was if I played sports. I told him softball. With no test or questions he told me that I had pulled a hamstring muscle.

Because he was the doctor I believed him, and now I knew what it was. He told me to get an ace bandage to wrap my thigh. I told him the pain had happened in my calf muscle not my thigh. He told me the pain could travel all over the leg. Once again he was the doctor and I believed him, and I now knew what it was. I asked no more questions.

While still in middle school, around 12- 14-years-old, during gym class a friend and I were running laps around the outside track as we always did. On our final lap of the day I told her that we should race to the finish line.

As we got closer to the finish line I told her let's go. She took off running. My mind was telling me to run, but my legs moved and wobbled like they were stuck in jell-o. When she reached the finish line she looked around for me.

She walked back towards me and asked what happened. I told her I was tired. I wasn't really tired, but how could I explain to her what just happened? I could not even explain to myself what had just happened. I was very perplexed.

JOHN 13:7 *"You do not realize now what I am doing, but later you will understand."*

<u>UNWELCOMED COMPANY</u>

My first job was in 1985. I was 18-years-old working as a cashier at HARDEE'S. It was a fun place to work and the customers were great. One day I went to work and I was made aware, by a customer, that my left eye was jumping up and down.

I had felt my eye jumping and twitching, but I did not know it was that noticeable.   I continued to work hoping everyone else would be more concerned about their orders than my eye.

This one guy was more concerned about my eye. His exact words, as he pointed at me were, "look at that little eye go!"   I was so embarrassed. I looked at him with nothing but hate in my heart until he got the message that I was not in the mood for his sarcasm, so he ordered his food and left.

After going home I saw my eye jumping the way my customers were seeing my eye. It made me realize that I needed to get my eye checked out. I made an appointment with my primary care physician.

He told me it was a nervous twitch. He gave me a prescription of Valium to take. I did not take it because my mom told me that I could get addicted to it. Getting addicted to Valium was not going to happen to me. Eventually, the problem with my eye just went away.

In 1988 I gave birth to my first daughter, Shannel. Four and half years later, in 1993, I gave birth to my second daughter, Cierra. After having my daughters I found myself becoming very tired and fatigued. I considered this to be what parents had to go through with having more than one child.

Within the next two years I would find out that being tired and fatigued were not the only things I would have to experience with having two children. The lack of sleep would play havoc with my eyesight.

My eye problems would become so problematic that I had no other choice but to go to an eye specialist to get a precise professional opinion. I was not prepared for the diagnosis the eye specialist would give me.

Becoming a little more concerned about my eye problem I made an appointment with an Eyes, Ears, Nose and Throat doctor. After they did some very extensive examinations the doctor informed me he could not find anything wrong.

He suggested that I should go to the hospital to have a MRI for something he thought could be MS. I became scared and began to cry. Those were words I had never heard of before.

The doctor got his female assistant to console me. The nurse then made an appointment for me to have the MRI done a few hours later. I left the doctor's office to go home so I could tell my mother. Just like a mother, my mom told me to pray and that everything would be fine.

With that boost of confidence I felt good about having the MRI. When I arrived to the hospital the nurse checked me in and took me to my room. As I got settled in I remembered my mom's words, "Pray". I started reciting the 23rd Psalm in the Bible. You know the one that begins, "The lord is my shepherd...."

When the prayer was finished I looked toward the ceiling and told GOD, "You said you would be there in my time of need." Foolishly I looked around the room to see if anything had moved to let me know that he was with me. Unfortunately I had not seen nor heard anything.

The nurse returned to tell me it was time to have the test done. When we got to the area to have the MRI the nurse asked me if I was claustrophobic. I told her no. She positioned me in the machine, placed a sheet across my chest, and a cloth across my eyes.

I was then glided into the machine. While I was having the test done, I had to listen to loud screeching, banging, and grinding sounds. I tried to drown them out by humming church songs. The next thing I am about to say may seem unreal to you because almost 20 years later I still can't believe it happened.

While in the machine I started to see a vision of a cloud of smoke. Instantly I thought the machine was on fire. I tried to take the cloth from over my eyes, but I couldn't move. The cloud of smoke started to get bigger and began to come towards me.

As it got closer to me it started to open up. I began to see this man in a white gown. He had a reddish color scarf wrapped around his neck and a sheep by his side. He said to me, "I am always with you". The man backed up with the sheep and the cloud faded away.

The nurse then glided me out of the machine for a moment to tell me that the doctor needed to have another test done. I did not want to go back into that crazy machine, but I was advised that I had to.

The nurse did not put the cloth over my eyes this time. I was glad she didn't because if what I was thinking happened to me again I was going to make sure I saw it and I was clear about what I saw.

I began to look around while I was lying in the machine. Nothing happened. I breathed a sigh of relief. Without any apparent warning it happened again. I saw the smoke, the cloud, and the man with the sheep.

This time the man pointed at me and said, "Remember, I am always with you." Immediately fades away. I was removed from the machine. The doctor returned with papers in hand and put x-rays on the screen. The results were in.

Let me introduce myself. My name is Multiple Sclerosis.

Psalm 27:1 "The Lord is my light and my salvation; who shall I fear? The Lord is the stronghold of my life; of whom shall I be afraid?"

UNFAMILIAR TERRITORY

In 1996 I was working a temporary job at Allstate Insurance Company as a Claims Processor. One morning I woke up to get ready for work. While in the bathroom brushing my teeth, as I was bent over the sink, my cheek felt kind of heavy.

When I stood up to look in the mirror I did not recognize myself. My eyelid was drooped down and my nose and lips were twisted on one side. I thought I had a stroke or something.

I called out of work and went to the hospital. I told them I had been diagnosed with MS in 1995. They started a plan to give me one hour IV steroids for a week. They placed the needle through a vein in my hand to administer the medicine.

I just knew things were going to be complicated confronting my co-workers the next day. Not only with the distortion of my face, but telling them that I had MS. The hospital kept the needle in my hand and I did not know what needed to be done to hide this at work. I decided to wear a glove.

My decision to wear a glove over my hand had made the situation even worse. The numerous sneaky stares from people became so apparent that I had to make up some type of lie in order to stop being the center of attention.

Just as I was instructed, I went to the hospital every day after work for a week to receive steroid treatment. After the week of steroids my face started to not look as twisted anymore. I had honestly started to think this was the end of MS. I could now begin to live as before.

Two years later with no encounters with my eye twitching or face distorting, I was on my way home from work one day and a familiar feeling from childhood came in my leg. I started thinking back to the nervous twitch in my eye that I had dealt with a decade ago and the mysterious twist in my face. In a second I knew there was a need for me to find a nerve and joint pain doctor.

It was in September 1998 when I found Mecklenburg Neurological Associates. Well, I didn't really find them I remembered them. I used to work there for a brief period as an Insurance Specialist.

I made an appointment with the doctor's office; not to get diagnosed because my diagnosis had already been determined. What I was looking for was a knowledgeable neurologist to instruct me on how to deal with the prognosis.

During my visit I saw my friend Sherri and some other familiar faces I used to work with. I was no longer going there as an employee, but as a patient. I saw my appointed doctor and I told him who, where, and when I got my diagnosis.

The doctor reports were requested from the hospital, which re-confirmed that I did indeed have bona fide Relapsing Remitting MS. I asked him what was going to happen to me. He told me that he didn't know and that I needed to tell him everything that had been going on with me.

He gathered information from me and decided to put me on a daily injection of Copaxone. This medicine was to slow down the number of exacerbations or attacks I was having. I hated having to get injections and now I would have to give myself one every day. I was also given a prescription for Lyrica to help deal with the pain.

During this time a nurse had to come to my house to show me how and where to give myself the injection. Taking the injections seemed like a waste of time to me. I had been under the impression that when I gave myself a shot that the pain would immediately go away. My pain did not go away like that. I had learned that was not how the injections were intended to work.

When I began taking the injections on my own it would take me almost 2 hours. It took me a while to get used to it. I believed my fear of doing it was making it harder than it really was. To this day I still do not like giving myself injections.

Bruising sometimes occurred when I took the injections in my thighs. When I injected myself in the arm it would hurt a lot. My arm would go limp and I had to wait for at least 15 minutes to regain feeling. I bruised there a lot too.

At this time my girls started to become suspicious of my daily actions, so I finally got the courage to try explaining my illness to them. I had to explain to them why mommy would shut herself up in her room and why she asked to be left alone. It was because my pain was so severe; I could not focus on my injections or even them.

How was I to explain why mommy got so tired that she couldn't take you to the park or spend quality time with you like she promised? It was because my body had shut down to where I was physically drained and too weak to move.

Those times when I would get so upset with you all for something as minor as not closing the box of Frosted Flakes all the way or not cleaning your room exactly when I told you to, etc.? It was because I was going through a state of depression and having anxiety attacks.

Remember when I used to ask both of you to hold my hands in the store when you were obviously old enough to walk by yourself? It was because I needed you all to help me to walk and not fall. I was naively too ashamed to use a cane or be in a wheelchair.

HEBREWS 12:2 *"It's for the joy of GOD that I endure."*

UNCERTAIN FUTURE

I continued to work for eight years after having the doctors diagnose me with MS in 1995. One day, in July 2003, I had a major attack at home. I called my neurologist who told me I needed to come into the office.

He could not detect the nature of the attack so he gave me a prescription of steroids. I had to take at least 10 pills a day, three times a day, for three 3 days. He also wrote me out of work for one week. After the week, I went back to the doctor to get an update. Another prescription of steroids was given. He wrote me out of work for a second week. No prognosis yet.

By this time my job wanted to know when I would be returning to work. I went to the neurologist for the third week feeling the same way I did the prior two weeks. I told him my job wanted to know my return date.

He checked me over and informed me that I needed to apply for disability. He could not specifically tell me when I would return to work. The nature of this particular attack was undetermined. My mouth quickly dropped open in utter disbelief. My last day of work was August 19, 2003.

After being diagnosed with MS, things never seemed to be the same anymore. I don't know if it was my own "why me?" low self esteem or if other people were starting to see and treat me differently.

Some of my friends, who knew I had MS, acted differently towards me when we were around others who they considered to be their normal friends. This was mainly during the time I was having an exacerbation or an attack.

Dating started to seem almost unattainable. Do I or do I not tell? If I told a guy in the beginning of us dating that I had MS, he would either not call again or he would make it seem as if I just told him that I had a contagious disease. Some of the ones I told in the beginning were fine until they witnessed an attack.

The guys who witnessed me have an attack would question why I was walking a certain way or why I was doing things so slowly. I knew then how that relationship was going to end up. It wasn't as if I withheld the truth from them. They just could not handle the truth. Even though I had told them about my condition and what it would sometimes do.

For the guys who I did not tell in the beginning I stopped calling them when I started to have an attack. I wanted to avoid the pain of being humiliated by them. At any age people can be cruel about things they don't understand.

If people were going to treat me as if I was out of the ordinary, then I will be screwed in this world. I began to feel hopeless, unworthy, and burdensome. I tried to let the people who knew me know that I was the same person they have always known by doing things to not embarrass other people or myself.

I would stop while walking to wait for an attack to run its course so I would not walk funny. I would put my cup down when my hands got the shakes so I would not spill my drink.

I would leave the room when my pain was so severe that it was written all over my face to not appear to be looking strange. I started not eating out in public a lot because I would sometimes get choked while swallowing my food.

What was I supposed to do or how was I supposed to act normal again when I knew I had no control over myself? No matter how I tried to cover it up MS kept finding a way of showing up.

I just wanted people to know that Lisa was still the same friendly, loving, caring, funny, and trusted person that they had grown to love. Only now I am Lisa who has MS. I was dealing with a situation that needed my undivided attention and their undivided understanding in such a way that I had no idea on how to handle it.

This was a very difficult time in my life. My exacerbations started out lasting only 5 minutes at a time. This was something I could manage. They gradually progressed to 45 minutes at a time. Occasionally they would happen more than once a day.

I could no longer try to cover up my illness. I started to become a hermit. I only dealt with outside world as needed. Such as going to doctor appointments, my daughters' school events, grocery shopping, getting gas, having maintenance done for my car, and going to the bank.

These were things everyday people did. When I did not have to do those things, I only sought to be with my family who knew and understood what I was going through. I tried to avoid any type of social activity.

My family knew when I was having trouble walking and they would advise me to rest. They knew if I got choked while eating to not laugh. If I forgot something they would not make me feel stupid.

When rounding corners I may bump a wall or lose my balance, they would ask if I was okay. I was tired of having to explain my entire life to other people. Just to have mistaken identity or be misunderstood.

I thought being in seclusion would be an alright way to live. That way of living started becoming too much of an obligation for me. It was a very dreary way to live. Every time I tried to get away from living this way, I was drawn back because I was ashamed.

It was as if I had given MS permission to take over my whole life. I can't do this, an attack may happen. I can't go there, an attack may happen. I can't meet this person, an attack may happen. What in the world was I suppose to do?

One night while in my room I was having a severe attack on the left side of my body. Then it had the audacity to attack the right side of my body at the same time. I was in insufferable pain all over. All I could think of was the electrical shocking pain and solitude being the way I would have to live for the rest of my life.

My medicine bottles were on the nightstand right beside me while these thoughts were going through my head. I grabbed them, poured some of them in my hand, and just when I was about to put them in my mouth to swallow them my youngest daughter Cierra screamed my name from the living room.

It startled me so bad that I dropped the pills to see what was wrong. She had dropped a mirror and had a piece of glass in her foot. I got the tweezers to start pulling the glass out of her foot hoping to get it all.

I was so focused on the situation with my daughter that I had forgotten about my own problem. I realized then that I was not only allowing MS to take over my life, but I was allowing having MS to try to kill me also.

When everything was situated with my daughter I went back in my room and picked up the medicine that I had dropped on my bed. I placed all the pills back in their bottles.

I began to notice this was not only about me. My girls needed their mother. A silent prayer for guidance was said to GOD and I heard a still small voice say to me, "it's not your time."

PROVERBS 14:15 "A *simple man believes anything, but a prudent man gives thought to his steps.*"

UNHAPPY HOLIDAYS

December 24, 2003 started out to be one of the best days of my life. I love Christmas time. I seemed to be on my very best behavior during this season. Nobody walked by without me smiling, waving, or giving an encouraging word. I normally would speak to everyone, but during this time, I was going out of my way to make sure everyone received a happy gesture from me.

My daughters, Shannel and Cierra, told me that I was embarrassing them. I told them that this is just who I was. A little later I began to notice that I was becoming a little too overly friendly, so I slowed down on the happy gestures tremendously. Not because of what my girls said, but because I started to feel a numbness and tingling in my fingers.

Trying not to let my girls figure out that something was wrong I held my right hand with my left hand as if rubbing them together. They were too busy noticing something else going on with me to mention my hand. My left eye was becoming small. As if it was trying to close.

The eye episode didn't last for long, but my fingers and hands remained numb. We continued shopping for a little while longer and then went home. I made a call to Mecklenburg Neurological and left a message. The doctor called me back to ask my symptoms. I told him everything that had happened.

He told me to continue taking my medicines and to pay close attention to what happened through the night. If I had no changes I was to call him and he would meet me at Mercy Hospital the next day. I started getting tired so we ate a quick dinner and turned in for the night.

When I woke to go to the bathroom the next morning I made an attempt to stand up. My body leaned towards the right. As I began to lean, I fell against my dresser. There was no feeling on my right side. My right side was paralyzed. I called out to my girls and they helped me to the living room couch. This was Christmas day.

My mother (Louise), my sisters (Eartha and Renee), and my niece and nephews came over to bring me dinner before I went to the hospital. We called my sister, Harriett, who lives in New Jersey on the phone to pray that everything went well for me.

I did not have an appetite so I could not enjoy the festivities. Standing up alone was still a problem. My daughters were continuing to help me go back and forth from wherever I was to the bathroom throughout the day. I made sure to get up only when necessary to not disturb them too much.

There were no changes throughout the day so I called the doctor. He told me he would meet me at the hospital. I phoned a male friend to drive me to the hospital. Upon arrival the hospital's hospitality department noticed me and they brought out a wheelchair.

Looking puzzled I wondered why I had to be wheeled in; my friend was there to assist me. I was told by the staff that they got the wheelchair for me because they noticed that I could barely maneuver myself or stand up. They did not want my friend to be another emergency incident while trying to balance me.

When I was wheeled to my room a nurse came in to take my vital signs and asked me if I needed anything. I told her no. After she got done checking me I put my jacket back on.

She looked at me smiling and said, "You really think you are leaving today?" I said yes after the visit I will. Looking straight at me she lets me know that I was going to be there for awhile.

My daughters were 10 and 15. I told her I couldn't stay. I had to get back home so I could take care of them. She asked me if I had family in town. My response was yes. She told me to call them to make arrangements for them to help me. I started sobbing and my friend began to comfort me.

My sisters along with my daughters came to the hospital. I told them my doctor will be giving me IV steroids and that I would be there for awhile so I would need their help with the girls. I brought up other family members who could help if they were not too busy.

Without hesitation my 15-year-old daughter, Shannel, said she has been around me enough to know how to take care of her and her little sister. I can't express to you how right before my eyes I began to see my oldest daughter become so mature.

My cousin, Shelitha, volunteered to keep my girls at her house. Once again Shannel said they would be fine. I could not tell them how long I would be in the hospital so family called my girls every day to make sure they had everything they needed. Thank God it was Christmas break. No school. That's when I finally started to realize this was going to be my home for awhile.

When I arrived at the hospital it was late in the afternoon. They were able to provide me with both lunch and dinner. I barely touched my juice. The nutritionist instructed me that even if the steroids helped, if I did not gain 10 pounds I could not be released.

My weight at the hospital was less than 100 lbs. I am 5'1. I was 105 pounds prior to this. My male friend had noticed that I had not been eating like I should have before this incident. I thought it was just because I was not hungry. I realized then that this was considered to be what you would call having a MS attack or exacerbation.

Normal daily hygiene was almost impossible to do in the hospital. I was right handed and the IV was in my left arm. I had to drag the IV machine back and forth like a cane to get to the sink to brush my teeth and wash my face.

Taking a shower was the worst. Basically all I could do was lean against the shower wall and let the warm water run down the front and back of my body while trying to maneuver the washcloth. Remember, my right side is completely numb. I had to try and force my right hand to work like it was supposed to.

Over time, the steroids started to slightly help my right side enough to where the nurse unplugged the IV from my hand in order for me to have many therapists come in my room to work on getting me back to the way I was before this unexpected exacerbation.

There was an occupational therapist who took me in the hallway to try an teach me to walk again, a speech therapist to teach me to talk without slurring, and a nutritionist to teach me how to eat three meals a day again. Oh, by the way, I was 36-years-old.

One night while in the hospital my nurse came in to check my pulse and left. After that another nurse came in with her. They started talking to each other. I asked if everything was okay. They told me my pressure is a little low.

A nurse then began to check my pulse every hour, and every hour it was getting lower. They called the doctor with Mecklenburg Neurological. He asked me how I was feeling. I told him cold and dizzy. I began to pray.

My doctor ordered some type of medication for me. You would think after that I became royalty. The staff was keeping such a tight watch over me. By morning my pulse was starting to get higher.

In the afternoon my pulse had become stable. That whole event was a very frightening ordeal for me. I felt as though that night was destined to happen; to will my mind and body to fight and not give up.

The next day my nurse informed me that I seemed better. I agreed. They removed the IV from the machine. My hands were more accessible to use while brushing my teeth, washing my face, going to the bathroom, and taking a shower.

After 6 days of intense occupational therapy, nutritional therapy, and speech therapy I was walking better without assistance, eating 3 meals a day and my words were understood more. The 7th day, New Years, I was able to go home.

MATTHEW 11:28 *"Come unto me all you who are weary, and burdened, and I will give you rest"*

UNFORTUNATE NEWS

On the following Monday a physical therapist came to my house so she could continue therapy for my independent walking. She said it may take from six months to a year before I got back to my regular activities. My therapist came by for two weeks and then told me that she could not come by anymore. Unaware of her comment I asked if my insurance had run out.

She told me that my insurance was fine. It was that I did not need her anymore. My response was yes I do! The therapist told me my body was responding to the therapy sooner than was expected. Her words to me were to continue the exercises she instructed and I would be fine. I did all of the exercises given to me faithfully both day and night.

The next day my daughter, Cierra, and I went to Walgreens. She was walking ahead of me. She turned around looking at me as I was approaching her and she said, "Mommy you're walking normal." I was very happy to hear a compliment again. That happy moment did not last long.

We checked the mailbox when we got home and I had received a letter in the mail threatening foreclosure. During this time I was in the process of filing for disability. No money was coming in. I had to think fast or everything I had worked and paid for was going to be left in the house once they pad locked my home.

You could imagine the stress I was dealing with at this time. I got the paper to look for houses to rent. I spotted one in an area I had always wanted to live in. A phone call, visit, completed application, and I had a house to rent in a month. I lived there from 2003 – 2006.

Feeling stressed I made an appointment with the neurologist. I cannot remember whether I had an attack or if my doctor wanted me to do a clinical trial, but he recommended chemotherapy. This medicine was supposed to be a prostate cancer drug, but appeared to work well on MS patients.

The therapy seemed to be working fine. I was not having any attacks. I went to my chemotherapy appointment one day, as normal, and something went wrong. While you are receiving therapy the nurses walk by to check on you.

A nurse had walked by and noticed my blood had gotten low. She phoned my neurologist to inform him. I received crackers and juice as I waited. Nothing could be done until they heard from the doctor. It took some time, but my doctor called back and told the nurse to discontinue the therapy.

I made an appointment with my doctor at a later date to find out what happened. He told me that he thought I had enough of the chemotherapy. If it was ever needed again I could get it. I was allowed 12 months of chemotherapy, but I had only used 6 months. It was good to know that it was not because I was having a more aggressive exacerbation.

PSALMS 46:1 *"GOD is our refuge and strength an ever-present help in trouble."*

<u>UNDYING FAITH</u>

By the summer of 2006, Shannel was about to graduate from high school and Cierra was a teenager. Going off to college was not something Shannel was looking forward to doing. It wasn't because of her grades; she had a 3.57 grade point average. It was because she knew how my constant agonizing attacks/exacerbations could change my attitude to where I would become very irritated, withdrawn, and not so pleasant to be around.

Cierra would now have to handle my onsets all alone. Shannel used to be the one to oversee things when I was in astonishing pain and when I wanted to be left alone. Now that she would be going off to college in another city she did not want her little sister to feel as if she was irrelevant to me when my attacks would happen. Shannel had found her own way of finding retreat when I was experiencing my painful attacks.

She would cry and confide in a close friend or family member that she felt as if she was the one being attacked because she felt as if there was nothing she could do to help me. Friends and family would advise her that, in her own way, she was helping me just by giving me the time I needed alone to cope with the severe attack.

Eventually, Shannel ended up going to UNC in Greensboro. She dropped out after a year due to financial woes, and worrying about how Cierra and I were doing at home. After being home for awhile she noticed how my exacerbations were being maintained well enough for her to go back to college. She decided she would go to a college in Charlotte, where she could work and provide assistance at home if needed.

I was still having my regular visits with the neurologist. During a visit in 2009 my doctor asked me if I was having any problems. One of the things I told him was that I was feeling a little depressed.

He prescribed me Wellbuterin which is an antidepressant. I took that for awhile, but noticed it was making me sick even if I had just eaten. I was supposed to take 2 tablets a day, but I decided to take 1 a day to see if that would stop the nausea. It did; as long as I had a full stomach.

My daughter, Cierra, was a junior in high school in 2010. I was on my way to take her to school and we had an argument in the car. It was over something very minor, but it made me very upset. When I got home I sat in my car for awhile. I turned the car off and closed the garage door.

My radio was off in my car and I heard a phone ring. I looked in the backseat to see if Cierra had left her cell phone. I did not see it. I heard the phone ring a total of three times as I looked for it. After I realized that it was not in the car, I went inside the house.

With my mind still preoccupied around my argument with Cierra, I went to my bedroom and started to think. Sitting on my bed I saw my medicine bottles on the nightstand. Déjà Vu. Once again I was contemplating suicide.

The phone rings. It was my daughter Shannel. She could tell I had been crying so I let her know how I was feeling and what I planned to do. She's crying softly, but in a calm voice tried to talk me out of it.

I did not want to hear what she is saying so I hung up. I put the pills in my hand. The bottle was turned to where I was reading the label. It said this medicine may cause drowsiness, nausea, *SUICIDAL THOUGHTS*, etc. If you had any of these symptoms call your doctor.

I phoned the doctor. He slowed me down enough to have a sensible conversation. He asked me if he called the Mental Health Department to make the appointment, would I go. I told him yes. He made the appointment while I was on hold.

Shannel called me again right after my conversation with the doctor. She begged me to go to the Mental Health Dept. I told her I would. Right after I hung up with her the phone rings again. It's my friend Denise. She tells me that Shannel had called her daughter, Brittany, crying about me and so Brittany called her. We talked for awhile until I was no longer confounded.

I never went to the Mental Health Department. Instead, I fell on my knees and went to the Father, Son, and Holy Spirit. An unseen phone in my car did not ring three times for nothing. I believed the Holy Spirit was unraveling my mind to let me know "you will hear your phone ring three times when you go in your house."

"This will be a sign to keep you from all hurt, harm, and danger. It will be up to you whether you take heed or not." I decided at that moment to not just be a hearer of the word, but a doer.

Another visit to my neurologist, to follow up on my recent attempted suicide, and he has me take another MRI test to see if there had been any more activity in my brain. The results came back and there had been no changes since my last MRI several years ago. This was a very good sign. After getting the results, I stopped taking the Wellbuterin.

In 2011, Cierra graduated high school with a 3.40 grade point average, and Shannel graduated from Kaplin College the same year. In 2014 Cierra also graduated from Kaplin College. It took us all some time to realize how my diagnosis of MS was more than any of us could have ever fathomed it to be. Thankfully we were able to rely on each other's strength to discover our own capabilities and restore our faith. The affliction used for harm in my life GOD designed it for good.

It is now 2015 and I continue my daily regimen of an injection of Copaxone 3 times a week, two Lyrica tablets twice a day, two Oybutynin tablets twice a day, one 4000 mg of vitamin D tablet, and one Lunesta tablet at night for sleep.

With continuation of this schedule I have not had a major attack or exacerbation since 2006. The right side of my body is still a little weak. I cannot stand, sit, or walk for long periods, but I still continue to retain mobility. I do not have to use a cane, wheelchair, or my daughter's assistance.

My left eye vision is somewhat blurry due to optic neuritis, but thank GOD I am still able to see and read things. I do not drive at night. That's okay. I am a morning person.

My cognitive memory is an issue at times to where I may have to write things down to remember them or I may sometimes repeat things. Not too often though. I can typically notice when I start doing these things and rectify myself.

The best thing to happen is that God's goodness and mercy has followed me and I have now with joy been in remission for the past 11 years. I will not say that these things will never happen again, but no matter what if GOD did it before he will do it again.

I could have let the diagnosis of MS consume my life, and it almost did. It's said that tests and trials come to make us strong. Clearly MS was my trial then and Philippians 4:13 was and is my strength now. From the beginning my mom told me to pray and that everything would be fine. I haven't stopped praying yet. I will never stop believing these powerful words from GALATIANS 2:20, "It is no longer I who live, but GOD lives in me."

I have been blessed with what I consider to be a very happy normal life and doing what I consider to be very normal things. I am socializing more with people outside of my family, eating out more in public with family and friends, and connecting more with men while no longer being afraid to disclose who I am. I had to come to the realization that I have MS, but I will not let MS have me.

I Corinthians 10:13 *"No temptation has overtaken you that is not common to man. God is faithful, and he will not let you be tempted beyond your ability, but with the temptation he will also provide the way of escape, that you may be able to endure it."*

50 by Lisa Norman

Lisa Norman: Biography

Lisa Norman is a native of Queens, New York, and currently resides in Charlotte, North Carolina. Lisa has two daughters (Shannel and Cierra) and one grandson (Daniel). Lisa has been inspired with writing and poetry since she was a teenager. She had her first poem, "In the Beginning," published in 1987 in an Anthology entitled, "On the Threshold of a Dream". Lisa wrote her first book, "The Wall," in September 1995. With no positive feedback from the writers she lost hope in her dream of ever becoming a writer/author. Her diagnosis of MS in November 1995 was her confirmation of lost hope. Not only in her dream of becoming a writer/author, but her dream of becoming the person GOD wanted her to be.

"My 18 year rollercoaster life with MS consisted of despair, turned into 'I think I can' then back down to hopelessness." Lisa's rollercoaster life experience revealed to her that if the enemy can control your mind, he can control your whole life. The veil that she was wearing over her face was not only keeping her from seeing herself, but it was keeping her from seeing GOD.

Lisa realized that living with MS consists of moment to moment dependence on GOD, being sensitive to his voice, her obedience to him, and testifying that she is his child.

"This is my journey." – Lisa Norman

www.ingramcontent.com/pod-product-compliance
Lightning Source LLC
Chambersburg PA
CBHW071647040426
42452CB00009B/1786